Melissa
<u>To</u>

Grandma Joy
<u>From</u>

Dec 25th/2016
<u>Date</u>

Dear Missy

I will be waiting
for my door bell to
ring ... And there
you will be with a
plate of cookies? say ...
Hi Grandma just
dropped by to
have Tea with
you ...

Mini Teatimes

Paintings by
Susan Rios

HARVEST HOUSE PUBLISHERS

EUGENE, OREGON

Mini Teatimes

Text Copyright © 2010 by Harvest House Publishers
Artwork Copyright © 2010 by Susan Rios

Published by Harvest House Publishers
Eugene, Oregon 97402
www.harvesthousepublishers.com

ISBN 978-0-7369-2667-6

Original artwork by Susan Rios. For more information regarding artwork featured in this book, please contact:

Susan Rios Designs
263 W. Olive Avenue, #274
Burbank, California 91502
(818) 571-7134 www.susanriosdesigns.com

Design and production by Garborg Design Works, Savage, Minnesota

Harvest House Publishers has made every effort to trace the ownership of all poems and quotes. In the event of a question arising from the use of a poem or quote, we regret any error made and will be pleased to make the necessary correction in future editions of this book.

All Scripture quotations are taken from the New King James Version. Copyright ©1982 by Thomas Nelson, Inc. Used by permission. All rights reserved.

Printed in China

10 11 12 13 14 15 16 /LP/ 10 9 8 7 6 5 4 3 2 1

Contents

Let the thankful heart sweep through the day and,
as the magnet finds the iron,
so it will find, in every hour, some heavenly blessings!

—HENRY WARD BEECHER

A Gracious Moment...

I have a close circle of friends that gathers for tea to celebrate any and every event, from birthdays to babies to "just because." What a treasure. Taking tea with friends puts you in a new state of mind. The conversations are about happy things. The pace is leisurely, and you feel your cares melt away as you rest in the present.

When I create my art, I like to imagine places that are beautiful, tranquil, and peaceful—places that my friends and I would enjoy. Some of the images in this gathering are of actual tea shops: Inn on Summer Hill, A Spot for Tea, Camellia Rose Tea Room, and Rose Tree Cottage. Imagining and discovering delightful places like these are part of the joy of tea.

To appreciate tea is to appreciate the moment. And to live the gracious art of tea is to extend those lovely feelings of gratitude beyond the tea table and into our everyday lives.

Susan Rios

NOW SERVING:
Tea and Gratitude

The act of taking tea invites us to a more profound awareness of what is beautiful and meaningful. We are able to notice delicious details like the hand-painted trim on an antique china cup, the melt-in-your-mouth texture of a fresh blueberry scone, and the scent of a hyacinth blossom in the centerpiece. One sip from a hot cup of tea and our hearts are filled with thanksgiving for the gifts in our daily lives—from friendships to blessings to trials.

Take a seat, slowly pour another cup of tea, and take in the aroma and the warmth of the amber liquid. Enjoy the pleasure of a life steeped in gratitude.

Pumpkin Tea Bars

I love pumpkin pie, and this is a quick and easy way to enjoy that flavor anytime!

CRUST:
yellow cake mix
(reserve 1 cup for
topping)
1 large egg
½ cup butter, softened

FILLING:
1 can (1 pound, 13 ounces)
pumpkin (not pumpkin
pie filling)
2 large eggs
⅔ cup evaporated milk

TOPPING:
1 cup yellow cake mix
½ cup sugar
1 teaspoon cinnamon
¼ cup butter, softened

Set aside 1 cup yellow cake mix for topping. For the crust, combine the remaining dry cake mix, egg, and butter. Press into the bottom of a 9 x 13-inch glass baking dish (a metal pan may take longer to bake). For the filling, combine canned pumpkin, eggs, and evaporated milk and mix well. Pour over prepared crust. For the topping, combine the cup of reserved cake mix, sugar, cinnamon, and butter and mix until crumbly. Sprinkle over filling. Bake at 350 degrees for 45 to 50 minutes or until crumbs are golden brown. Cool completely before cutting into bars.

If the only prayer you ever say in your
entire life is thank you, it will be enough.

—MEISTER ECKHART

As flowers carry dew-drops, trembling on the edges of the petals, and ready to fall at the first waft of wind or brush of bird, so the heart should carry its beaded words of thanksgiving; and at the first breath of heavenly flavor, let down the shower, perfumed with the heart's gratitude.
—HENRY WARD BEECHER

Gratitude is the memory of the heart.

—JEAN BAPTISTE MASSIEU

10

Stands the church
clock at ten to three?
And is there honey
still for tea?

—RUPERT BROOKE

No matter what's going on in
my life, it always goes better
when I focus on all that I'm
grateful for. Even adversity can
be an opportunity, if you find
the blessing in it.

—SUSAN RIOS

11

NOW SERVING:
Tea and Bliss

Good friends warm the heart and inspire us to be better, happier, and more generous in our giving and living. A day brightened by time spent with a dear friend is divine. A conversation sprinkled with laughter is bliss. We know this sensation well from the burst of delight that comes over us when we sip that first cup of tea. Suddenly flowers are graced with richer hues, the tasks before us seem possible, and our future looks bright.

Bliss lets us dismiss the small irritations of life so that we can indulge in the sweet flavor of life's offerings. Whether you choose chamomile, Earl Grey, or chai, fill your cup and fill your day with love, faith, hope, and joy.

Blueberry Crumble

1 cup oats
1 cup brown sugar, firmly packed
1 cup all-purpose flour
½ cup unsalted butter, melted
6 cups blueberries

Combine oats, sugar, and flour. Add melted butter and toss with fingertips until crumbly. Place berries in a 9 x 13-inch casserole dish. Spread crumbled mixture over berries and bake 45 to 60 minutes at 350 degrees until bubbles around the edges appear thick.

Vegetable Frittata

14 large eggs
1½ cups heavy cream
1 tablespoon salt
½ teaspoon chili flakes
1 medium zucchini,
    shredded
12 mushrooms, sliced
1 cup green onions, sliced
1 red bell pepper, diced
2 cups corn
1½ cups fresh spinach,
    blanched and drained
1½ cups cheddar cheese
Garnish: Parmesan cheese,
    chives, and crumbled,
    crisply cooked bacon

In a large bowl, combine eggs, cream, salt, and chili flakes and beat well. Add vegetables and 1 cup cheddar cheese and mix well. Grease a large, ovenproof skillet and pour the mixture into the skillet. Sprinkle the remaining ½ cup cheddar cheese on top and bake at 350 degrees for 35 minutes or until set. Sprinkle plates with Parmesan cheese, chives, and crumbled bacon. Place a slice of frittata on garnishments and serve.

The path to heaven passes through a teapot.

—ANCIENT PROVERB

Happiness seems made to be shared.

—PIERRE CORNEILLE

One sip of this will bathe the drooping spirits in delight, beyond the bliss of dreams.

—MILTON

I've discovered that I feel the most joy when I'm totally in the present moment, appreciating it for what it is. Sometimes just noticing a beautiful tree or a child's wonderful smile brings me absolute joy.

—SUSAN RIOS

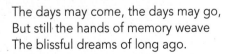

The days may come, the days may go,
But still the hands of memory weave
The blissful dreams of long ago.

—GEORGE COOPER

Friendship is the golden thread that ties the heart of all the world.
—JOHN EVELYN

Oh the experience of this sweet life.
—DANTE

Ecstasy is a glass full of tea and a piece of sugar in the mouth.
—ALEXANDER PUSHKIN

19

Tea and Renewal

It has long been touted that what pours from the spout of a teapot is filled with healing properties. Green tea is said to aid the cardiovascular and immune systems and help with cholesterol levels. Rosehips tea is an herbal tea high in vitamin C. White tea is filled with potent antioxidants. And all this goodness doubles when we share a cup with a friend!

Don't forget tea's wonders for your emotional well-being. When your mood or perspective needs a boost of energy and a little extra clarity, the hope and generosity of teatime is, without question, a balm for the soul.

Sissy's Lemon Bars

My friend Sissy worked as a caterer and perfected this yummy lemon bar. If there are any leftovers (doubtful), store in the refrigerator.

CRUST

2 cups all-purpose flour
½ cup powdered sugar
1 cup butter

FILLING

5 eggs
2 cups granulated sugar
¾ cup lemon juice
2 teaspoons freshly grated lemon peel
¼ cup all-purpose flour
½ teaspoon baking powder

CRUST

Sift flour and powdered sugar. Cut in butter until mixture clings together (you can use a food processor). Press this mixture into a greased 13 x 9-inch glass baking dish. Bake at 350 degrees for 25 minutes or until lightly browned around the edges. Let cool while making the filling.

FILLING

Beat eggs, granulated sugar, lemon juice, and peel until thick and lemon-colored. Sift flour and baking powder together and fold gently into egg mixture. Pour over baked crust. Bake at 350 degrees for 25 minutes or until the filling is set and forms a thin sugar crust with lightly browned edges. When cool, sprinkle with sifted powdered sugar and cut into small squares.

If you are cold,
    tea will warm you;
If you are too heated,
    it will cool you;
If you are depressed,
    it will cheer you;
If you are exhausted,
    it will calm you.

—WILLIAM GLADSTONE

We have to take time for ourselves and do something that fills our souls. Tea-time gives us a chance to appreciate great company, delicious food, and beautiful surroundings—that's about as good as it gets!

—SUSAN RIOS

Health and cheerfulness make beauty.

—CERVANTES

24

We must always change, renew, rejuvenate ourselves.

— JOHANN WOLFGANG VON GOETHE

The effect of tea is cooling and as a beverage it is most suitable. It is especially fitting for persons of self-restraint and inner worth.

—LU YU

Genius is the ability to renew one's emotions in daily experience.

—PAUL CEZANNE

Drinking a daily cup of tea will surely starve the apothecary.

—CHINESE PROVERB

NOW SERVING:
Tea and Style

Tea lets us express our sense of style. Some love their tea served in Victorian fashion with china displayed on a white linen tablecloth. Others prefer a casual tea that requires only a comfy chair by the window and a sturdy mug filled to the brim. Your season must-have might be an afternoon spent with friends seated on graceful wrought iron chairs under a striped awning that reminds you of a European sidewalk café. It's all about your personal style.

When you choose black tea with sugar and saffron from a tea menu, you'll know that your inner designer has emerged. But whatever tea captures your fancy, take it with a splash of personality in every cup!

Frozen Cranberry Salad

This has become a tearoom favorite! We serve it with all of our English lunch plates.

8 ounces cream cheese, softened
½ cup mayonnaise
1 cup granulated sugar
2 (12-ounce) cans jellied cranberry sauce
2 cups heavy whipping cream
1 cup powdered sugar

In a large mixing bowl, combine cream cheese, mayonnaise, and sugar using the whip attachment on the mixer. Whip until smooth. Add cranberry sauce and continue mixing until smooth. In a separate bowl, combine heavy cream and powdered sugar and whip to medium stiff peaks. Fold whipped cream mixture into cranberry mixture until fully combined. Scoop cranberry salad into individual cups and place in freezer for 1 hour or until frozen. Serve chilled with dollop of whipped cream. Enjoy!

The tea ceremony requires years of training and practice… yet the whole of this art, as to its detail, signifies no more than the making and serving of a cup of tea. The supremely important matter is that the act be performed in the most perfect, most polite, most graceful, most charming manner possible.

—LAFCADIO HEARN

If man has no tea in him, he is incapable of understanding truth and beauty.

—JAPANESE PROVERB

White Chocolate Bread Pudding

We use our leftover croissants for this recipe. Delicious!

3 cups whipping cream
10 ounces white chocolate
1 cup milk
½ cup sugar
2 eggs
8 egg yolks
Croissant bread or 1 loaf
French bread, sliced in
¼-inch pieces and dried
in oven.

Heat the cream in a double boiler and add the white chocolate. When the chocolate is melted, remove from heat. In a double boiler, heat the milk, sugar, eggs, and egg yolks until warm. Blend the egg mixture into the cream and chocolate mixture.

Place the bread in a greased 9 x 13-inch baking pan. Pour half of the mixture over the bread and let settle for a while, making sure the bread soaks up all the mixture. Top with the rest of the mixture. Cover with aluminum foil and bake at 275 degrees for 1 hour. Remove the foil and bake for an additional 15 minutes until the top is golden brown.

SAUCE:

8 ounces white chocolate
3 ounces heavy cream

Gently melt the white chocolate in a double boiler. Remove from heat and mix in heavy cream. Spoon over bread pudding.

When you sit down to a beautifully set table, sip a good brew from thin-lipped teacups, and enjoy delicious sandwiches and pastries, it is like taking a mini-vacation from "real life."

—SUSAN RIOS

The Baroness found it amusing to go to tea; she dressed as if for dinner. The tea-table offered an anomalous and picturesque repast; and on leaving it they all sat and talked in the large piazza, or wandered about the garden in the starlight.

—HENRY JAMES

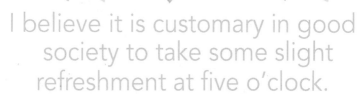

I believe it is customary in good society to take some slight refreshment at five o'clock.

—OSCAR WILDE

The ornament of a house is the friends who frequent it.

—RALPH WALDO EMERSON

She poured out Swann's tea, inquired "Lemon or cream?" and, on his answering "Cream, please," said to him with a laugh: "A cloud!" And as he pronounced it excellent, "You see, I know just how you like it." This tea had indeed seemed to Swann, just as it seemed to her; something precious, and love has such a need to find some justification for itself, some guarantee of duration, in pleasures which without it would have no existence and must cease with its passing.

—MARCEL PROUST

The privileges of the side-table included the small prerogatives of sitting next to the toast, and taking two cups of tea to other people's one.

—CHARLES DICKENS

I love you

NOW SERVING:
Tea and Celebration

Every celebration in life deserves…well, a celebration! When we honor milestones, holidays, achievements, dreams, and triumphs over difficulties in our lives and in the lives of those we love, we welcome joy to the table. Plan a tea for an occasion coming up on your horizon—a birthday or graduation, a bridal or baby shower, a friend's new job or new home. Imagine Easter laced with the pastel colors of spring and a cup of white tea with a sprig of mint. Envision a Mother's Day with floral bouquets and champagne glasses brimming with iced cranberry-green tea.

Through the timeless ritual of savoring and sharing, tea adds depth and loveliness to every occasion. Let the wonder of this new day be reason enough to celebrate with tea!

Angel Clouds

These melt-in-your-mouth cookies have many other names, such as Russian Tea Cakes or Snowballs, but we always call them Angel Clouds because they are as light as a cloud and as delicately sweet as an angel's kiss.

1 cup butter, softened
1 teaspoon vanilla
½ cup powdered sugar
2¼ cups all-purpose flour

½ teaspoon salt
¾ cup pecans, finely chopped
2 cups powdered sugar

Cream butter, vanilla, and ½ cup powdered sugar until light and creamy. Sift together flour and salt and stir in pecans. Gently mix with butter mixture until just combined—do not over-mix. Roll into 1-inch balls and place on greased baking sheet about 1 inch apart. Bake for 12 to 15 minutes or until lightly browned. As soon as you can handle the hot cookies, roll them in the 2 cups of powdered sugar. Immediately reroll them a second time and then let them cool completely. They will taste better the next day, but they rarely last that long!

Rejoice in
the things
that are
present;
all else
is beyond
thee.

—MICHEL DE MONTAIGNE

Fudge Drops

These brownie-like cookies are almost like eating candy. They are quick and easy and perfect for any celebration. And because they are not baked, they are great to make in the summer—no need to heat up your kitchen!

½ cup butter
2 cups sugar
½ cup milk
4 tablespoons cocoa
1 teaspoon vanilla
½ cup peanut butter
2 cups quick cooking oats
1 cup chopped nuts

(I also add ½ cup coconut and ½ cup raisins, but you can add any chopped, dried fruit you like. Cranberries? Apricots?)

Mix the butter, sugar, milk, and cocoa together in a 2-quart, heavy saucepan. Stir occasionally to prevent burning and bring to a full rolling boil. Boil for 1½ minutes. Remove from heat and add the vanilla. Stir in the rest of the ingredients until well blended. Drop by teaspoonfuls onto wax paper. Let cool and enjoy!

39

A thing of beauty is a joy forever.

—JOHN KEATS

What strong medicinal, but rich, scents from the decaying leaves! The rain falling on the freshly dried herbs and leaves, and filling the pools and ditches into which they have dropped thus clean and rigid, will soon convert them into tea—green, black, brown, and yellow teas, of all degrees of strength, enough to set all Nature a-gossiping.

—HENRY DAVID THOREAU

Friends—they are kind to each other's hopes. They cherish each other's dreams.

—HENRY DAVID THOREAU

Love is time and space, measured by the heart.

—MARCEL PROUST

Rejoice always, pray without ceasing,
in everything give thanks.

—THE BOOK OF FIRST THESSALONIANS

41

NOW SERVING:
Tea and Comfort

We all need a little comfort now and then. How wonderful that we can find it in the refuge of tea. Our cup, warm in our hands, doesn't ask questions. It merely is there for us. The familiarity of our favorite tea soothes us instantly with its aroma and flavor. This comfort embraces us like a cashmere throw or a glowing fire. Even beneath the sunny skies of summer, we benefit from the inner warmth of a moment wrapped in peace, stillness, and refreshment.

Take a personal day and make yourself a pot of orange pekoe, curl up with a favorite book, and enter the solace and the sanctuary of tea.

Swedish Pound Cake

CAKE

1 cup margarine
2 cups sugar
2 cups flour
5 eggs
1 teaspoon vanilla
1 cup semisweet chocolate
    chips
1 cup pecans, chopped

*Cream together margarine
and sugar. Add eggs all at
once. Add vanilla and then
flour. Mix well. Add chocolate chips and pecans. Pour
into 2 loaf pans and bake at
325 degrees for 1 hour.*

GLAZE

¾ cup sugar
¼ cup margarine
¼ cup water
1 teaspoon almond
    flavoring

*Combine sugar, margarine,
and water and boil for 3
minutes. Remove from heat
and add almond flavoring.
Pour glaze over completely
cooled cake.*

The cozy fire is bright and gay.
The merry kettle boils away
And hums a cheerful song.
I sing the saucer and the cup;
Pray, Mary, fill the teapot up.
And do not make it strong.

—BARRY PAIN

[I am a] hardened and shameless tea drinker, who has for twenty years diluted his meals only with the infusion of this fascinating plant; whose kettle has scarcely time to cool; who with tea amuses the evening, with tea solaces the midnight, and with tea welcomes the morning.

—SAMUEL JOHNSON

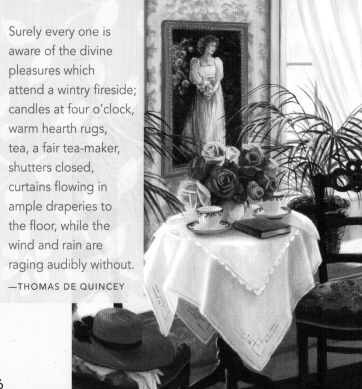

Surely every one is
aware of the divine
pleasures which
attend a wintry fireside;
candles at four o'clock,
warm hearth rugs,
tea, a fair tea-maker,
shutters closed,
curtains flowing in
ample draperies to
the floor, while the
wind and rain are
raging audibly without.

—THOMAS DE QUINCEY

Tortellini Soup

Combine the following ingredients in a large pot:

5 cups Italian flavored crushed tomatoes

4 (10.5-ounce) cans chicken broth

4 (10.5-ounce) cans beef broth

1 large bok choy, chopped

5 medium to large potatoes, peeled and quartered

5 carrots, peeled and sliced

In a separate pot combine:

3 pounds bulk Italian sausage

2 medium onions, chopped

water, enough to cover sausage and onions

1 cup butter

12 cups water

½ (.6-ounce) jar Italian seasoning

3 (9-ounce) packages of tortellini

Boil sausage and onions. Drain and let cool. Crumble sausage. Add crumbled sausage and onions to broth mixture in large pot. Add butter, 12 cups water, and Italian seasoning. Simmer for eight hours. Add tortellini 40 minutes before serving. Sprinkle with grated Parmesan cheese.

We've been friends for so long, when did we start?
Was there ever a time you weren't in my heart?

—REVEREND MARY BETH SPEER

Hope is the dream
of the waking man.

—FRENCH PROVERB

What part of confidante has that poor teapot played
ever since the kindly plant was introduced among
us. Why myriads of women have cried over it, to be
sure! ...Nature meant very kindly...when she made
the tea plant; and with a little thought, what series
of pictures and groups the fancy may conjure up and
assemble round the teapot and cup.

—WILLIAM MAKEPEACE THACKERAY

The most I can do for my friend is simply to be his friend. I have no wealth to bestow on him. If he knows that I am happy in loving him, he will want no other reward. Is not friendship divine in this?

—HENRY DAVID THOREAU

The more I move toward the experience of serenity, the more serenity moves toward me.

—REVEREND MAUREEN HOYT

Where there's tea there's hope.

—SIR ARTHUR PINERO

49

NOW SERVING:
Tea and Inspiration

How incredible that a simple liquid, created by brewing dried leaves, can inspire the best in people and in life! The many tributes to tea found in art, cultural traditions, and literature are evidence to this phenomenon. Of course, the only proof we need is the soothing, refreshing, and uplifting experience we have with tea in our daily lives. With each sip, consider how tea is one of your blessings. It can inspire creativity, hospitality, community, stillness, conversation, and gratitude.

As you create your own tea rituals to infuse your life with goodness, you'll long to share tea with others. This is tea's greatest inspiration.

Dolly's Carrot Cake

Joyce was my stepmom's name, but my dad always called her Dolly. Our family loved her carrot cake almost as much as we loved her.

2 cups flour
3 teaspoons baking powder
1½ teaspoons baking soda
1 teaspoon salt
2 teaspoons cinnamon
2 cups sugar
1¼ cups oil
4 eggs
2 cups carrots, grated
    and lightly packed
1 (8¼-ounce) can crushed
    pineapple, drained
    (reserve drained liquid)
½ cup nuts, chopped
½ cup raisins (optional)

Sift flour, baking powder, baking soda, salt, and cinnamon together into a large bowl. Add sugar, oil, and eggs; mix well. Stir in carrots, drained pineapple, and nuts. Turn into a well-greased 10-inch tube pan, bundt pan, or whatever shaped pan you like. Preheat oven to 350 degrees and bake for 50 to 60 minutes or until a toothpick inserted near the center comes out clean. Cool 10 minutes in pan, then

turn onto rack to cool completely. Frost with frosting of
your choice—cream cheese
frosting is perfect! Or serve
it plain or with a dusting of
powdered sugar.

Easy Cream Cheese Frosting
Combine reserved liquid
from canned crushed
pineapple with 8 ounces
softened cream cheese,
2½ cups sifted powdered
sugar and 1 teaspoon real
vanilla. Beat until very
smooth and glossy. This will
be more like a thick glaze
than a traditional frosting.
Pour over the cooled cake
and let it drip down the
sides.

Into the house
where joy lives,
happiness will
gladly come.

—JAPANESE PROVERB

I am in no way
interested in
immortality,
but only in the
taste of tea.

—LU TUNG

53

Teatime is by its very nature a combination of small luxuries arranged in social symmetry. And although tea for one is certainly a fine thing, the addition of a circle of dear friends to share it with ensures the whole is larger than its parts.

—AUTHOR UNKNOWN

Sweets to the sweet.

—WILLIAM SHAKESPEARE

My whole life is about inspiration; getting and giving. Many people and things inspire me, and I need that in my life as much as breathing.

—SUSAN RIOS

Do not forget to entertain strangers, for by so doing some have unwittingly entertained angels.

—THE BOOK OF HEBREWS

There is nothing like a dream to create the future.

—VICTOR HUGO

There is a great deal of poetry and fine sentiment in a chest of tea.

—RALPH WALDO EMERSON

NOW SERVING:
Tea and Garden Pleasures

The roses climb skyward on the trellis. A meandering path leads you to a table adorned with a porcelain tea set and a basket of pastries. There are so many pleasures to be found in Creation's tea room. Share them with others in simple ways. Host a Sunday picnic of cucumber sandwiches, potato salad, and a pomegranate infusion. Gather your family for outdoor games and tall glasses of satisfying iced tea. Invite a friend along on a trail walk and share a thermos full of ginger tea and great conversation.

The pleasures of tea reap an abundant harvest during every season of our journey. We need only to plant joy and kindness and to watch for the sprouts of new life along the way.

Cranberry and Apricot Tea Cake

This is a lovely recipe for an autumn tea.

1 cup sugar
1¾ cups all-purpose flour
½ cup butter
½ teaspoon soda
1 egg
½ teaspoon salt
¼ cup dried apricots,
    chopped
½ teaspoon baking powder
¼ cup dried cranberries,
    chopped
6 tablespoons milk

Cream butter and sugar until light in color. Add egg and blend thoroughly. Sift dry ingredients over apricots and add in stages. Stir in milk. Bake in greased 9-inch square pan at 350 degrees for 15 minutes. Remove from oven and spread with topping:

TOPPING
½ cup shredded coconut
¼ cup chopped dried
    apricots
¼ cup dried cranberries
½ cup brown sugar
2 tablespoons butter,
    softened

*After spreading topping
on cake, bake another
25 to 30 minutes or until
done. Cool in pan on rack.*

The heart hath its own
memory like the mind,
And in it are enshrined the
precious keepsakes.

—HENRY WADSWORTH
LONGFELLOW

*Let us be grateful
to people who make
us happy: they are
the charming gardeners
who make our souls
blossom.*

—MARCEL PROUST

Plum Cheese and Black Walnut Sandwiches

This is a favorite sandwich on Valentine's Day!

2 (8-ounce) packages Philadelphia Cream Cheese

1 ripe purple plum, seeded and cut in 6 to 8 sections

½ cup black walnuts

Raisin bread, sliced thin

In a food processor, cream the cheese and plum until nearly smooth. Add black walnuts and pulse until finely chopped and evenly distributed. Remove the crusts from the raisin bread and spread with cream cheese mixture. Cut with a heart-shaped cookie cutter or into triangle shapes and serve.

If the sight of the blue skies fills you with joy, if the simplest things of nature have a message that you understand, rejoice, for your soul is alive.

—ELEANORA DUSE

My
friends
are my
estate.

—EMILY DICKINSON

Tea is drunk to

forget the din of

the world.

—T'IEN YIHENG

May flowers always line your path and sunshine light your day. May songbirds serenade you every step along the way. May a rainbow run beside you in a sky that's always blue. And may happiness fill your heart each day your whole life through.

—IRISH BLESSING

I always fear that creation will expire before teatime.

—REVEREND SYDNEY SMITH

Hope is the only bee that makes honey without flowers.

—ROBERT INGERSOLL

Never lose an opportunity of seeing anything that is beautiful; for beauty is God's handwriting—a wayside sacrament. Welcome it in every fair face, in every fair sky, in every fair flower, and thank God for it as a cup of blessing.

—RALPH WALDO EMERSON

Recipes from featured tea houses were graciously provided courtesy of the following:

INN ON SUMMER HILL
Summerland, California
www.innonsummerhill.com

CAMELLIA ROSE TEA ROOM & GIFTS
Plant City, Florida
www.camelliarose.com

A SPOT FOR TEA
Oklahoma City, Oklahoma
www.aspotfortea.com

ROSE TREE COTTAGE
Pasadena, California
www.rosetreecottage.com